But Let's Not Be Maudlin

Poems
and
Drawings

by
Joanne Mellin

191 Bank Street
Burlington Vermont 05401

Acknowledgments

I would like to thank the editors of the following publications, in which three of these poems previously appeared, sometimes in different versions:

Burlington Poetry Journal, Volume I: "Yoga Moment"
The Mountain Troubadour: "Good Luck", "Progression"

I am grateful to the women in my poetry groups, stellar poets all, who inspire me to keep on writing; to Mary Jane Dickerson, my poetry mentor, Marshall Witten, and Bob Hannan, who all helped me in this effort.

Marian Willmott's steadiness and expertise have been a godsend.

And a special thank you to Geof Hewitt, my editor, who has been invaluable in guiding me through the process of finally making this book a reality.

Author photo by Pat Spielman.
Photo of author's mother by the author.
Book design by Marian Willmott.

But Let's Not Be Maudlin
ISBN: 978-0-9776458-1-1
Copyright © 2017 by Joanne Mellin
All rights reserved.

This book is dedicated to my mother, Ramona T. Otis

Sunday Night

Make use of the things around you.
This light rain
Outside the window, for one,
This cigarette between my fingers,
These feet on the couch.
The faint sound of rock-and-roll,
The red Ferrari in my head.
The woman bumping
Drunkenly around in the kitchen…
Put it all in,
Make use.

Raymond Carver

"But we aren't a glum lot."

Bill W.
Alcoholics Anonymous

Contents

1
Bereft	11
Home Rule	13
Wilder, VT	15
Progression	16
Fool	18
Hard Cases	20
A Safe Distance	22

2
Playing Possum	25
Get a Grip	26
What's in a Name	28
Good Luck	30
Lament	31
9/12/01	33

3
Life	37
Self-Seeking	38
Self Esteem	39
Reprieve	40
Oh Happy Day	41
A Day at the Beach	42
OK So I'm Not a Genius	43
Like Life	45
Voices	47
Bare Ground	48

4

Therapy	53
Love Sick	55
Seeing the Light	56
All Is Not Lost	58
Lower Companion	60
The Guilty Ones	62
Some People Need To Be Taught a Lesson	63
On This First Hot Day in April	64
Haunted	66
Substitution	68
Drunks and Fools	69

5

Dream On	73
Let's Face It	75
Window-Box, Snack Mix	76
Yoga Moment	78
Windows	79
The Bright Side	80
Lay Lady Lay	81

1

Bereft

I'm in the kind of mood
in which it gives me great satisfaction
to cut and slice vegetables –
I make a salad for supper.

I am pouting,
something I've always been good at.
I can hear Mother even now, saying
"Get that look off your face!"
I try to be upbeat, but sometimes
gravity takes over, pulls everything down.
It's a law that's hard to break.

No more *Bachelorettes in Alaska* on TV,
the final episode was last week.
Rebecca, the prettiest and most popular,
was left bereft at Proposal Point.
You should have seen her reaction –
I wanted to tell her to get that look off her face.

It might be fun to be a Bachelorette in Alaska,
but I'd probably be disqualified
for having been married three times.
How about "Widows in Wyoming"?
I could have a horse, go trail riding.
Growing up I was good at it,
spending summers at my aunt and uncle's farm,
in the saddle every day, smelling like horse sweat,
carried away.

My favorite horse was Prince –
if I called to him in the pasture

he'd come running.
He ran away with me once,
on the way back to the barn,
heading for a five-foot fence.
I was riding bareback with just a halter
but pulled his head around until he swerved
and galloped through the apple orchard
while I laid my head against his sweaty neck
to avoid the whipping branches.
He was a handful.

Back home for the school year
I got a letter from my cousin.
Prince broke his leg and had to be shot.
Then our old dog Patrick was killed;
lame and deaf, he limped into the street
in front of a car.
When he was young he was a rascal,
running away for days at a time,
coming home roguish and unrepentant
after I'd given up hope.

Nana used to tell me when I was little,
"Smile and the world smiles with you, weep
and you weep alone."
So let's not be maudlin –
it's almost time for *Survivor*.

Home Rule

Remember
when I longed to be alone?
Well I must have done something right
because now I am.

Remember
when my husband would ask me
What's for dinner?
and we had to eat at six every night?
Now, I can eat shredded wheat with bananas
for supper at ten if I want to.

And I can be silent.
Remember
when Daddy would get angry?
Did you hear what I said? Answer me!
And I'd have to force a reluctant yes
into the big space between us,
trying to gauge just how softly,
how defiantly I could say it
without provoking him further.
Now, I can go all day
and not open my mouth
if I don't feel like it —
though I always talk to the cat
so he won't think I'm mad
at him.

It's time to eat right now
because I'm hungry,
and tonight I'm serving myself

melted extra-sharp cheddar
on a sesame bagel,
with tomato slices, hot sauce,
and garlic powder.

And I don't worry about
garlic breath.

Wilder, VT

I've been thinking
of that summer in Wilder, 1959,
Jennifer and I riding down a deserted dirt road,
me on my cousin Mitchell's horse,
mine to ride now that Mitch was on to
more exciting things.
"Birthday" was a chunky chestnut
with a big white face and a placid disposition.
He took it in stride when
we picked tiger lilies from the roadside
and twined them into our horses' bridles,
polka-dotted orange flowers leading the way,
nodding in rhythm with the horses' steps.

Mitchell was my favorite person.
When we were little
I thought we'd get married,
but now, a year older than me,
he had other interests,
like drinking and wrecking cars.
I craved his attention so much that
when we were roughhousing in the barn
with the neighborhood kids
and he socked me in the eye by mistake,
I didn't even mind.
He was horrified,
so contrite, so solicitous and sweet —
I lapped it up!
It was the highlight of that summer
with my aunt and uncle and
my late, my favorite, cousin Mitchell.

Progression

I'd like to forget Freddy.
After all it's been thirty years
since he kissed me
in Kelton's horse barn.

I used to follow him around,
stand next to him
while he groomed the ponies,
help him put up fence in the back pasture,
and that day he finally noticed me,
said he wanted to take me on a date.

Afterwards I waited and waited on Nana's porch,
pretending to read on the red chaise lounge,
waiting for his maroon and white Ford to turn
into the driveway…

Then I heard he'd had to get married,
and you'd think that was that,
but twenty years later my cousin told me
that he was divorced and living nearby;
our one-night reunion ended
when his brother surprised us in bed –
so sordid, so disappointing,
when what I'd really wanted was
the sweetness of his unexpected kiss
in the quiet dusty barn.

The last time I saw him was ten years later
across the counter of the nurses' station
where I worked as a ward clerk.
He'd come to visit someone,

we spoke briefly,
he was close enough for me
to smell the booze on his breath at 10:00 a.m.,
and you'd think that was that;
poor Freddy.
Yes, you'd think that was that.

Fool

Now I know what it's like
to be so engrossed in a book
that you sit for hours reading
outside in the sun, heedless,
forgetting the sunscreen,
until your legs and feet
are sunburned
a deep, angry red.

Not on purpose
like in my teens,
slathered with a mixture of
iodine and baby oil,
at the pool with my friends
watching the boy I loved
do the Butterfly.

What a fool.

There's a photo of me
dancing with him at a party,
grinning at the camera,
happy happy happy;
but not for long,
he never called after that.

It was all about boys then,
whether they liked me
or not,
the power I gave them.

Now there's no one I need
to wonder about.

Hopefully the painful burn will fade
without that ugly peeling;
I'm not holding my breath.

Hard Cases

Housebound by a blizzard,
Mother and I work on
an impossible jigsaw puzzle
and reminisce about the bases
where we were stationed.

We talk about Charleston,
where Thurmon Munson,
the bully with a BB gun,
shot a baby squirrel out of the
magnolia tree,
and his dog Nana snatched
my brother's pet turtle from her aquarium
in the garden.
We found her in his family's trashcan
with a cracked shell, barely alive,
and though Daddy tried to patch her up
with black electrical tape
it was too late.

I ask if she remembers
Kenny B. Fatkin,
the bad boy in Arlington
we weren't allowed to play with,
who smashed a woods turtle against a tree,
and sicced his white bulldog
on our spaniel, Patrick.
His mother had a hump and
his schizophrenic father
roamed the streets at night,
cursing at the moon.

Then there was Norfolk and
neither of us can recall the name
of the delinquent with rotten teeth,
who laughed when his Scottish terrier
bit my sister in the leg;
who stole her bike and attacked it
with a sledge hammer,
leaving it mangled and useless.
Such a wretched, angry boy,
just like his father
the Police Chief.

Whenever I go hiking
I scan the woods and streams
in search of turtles;
I just want to see one up close again,
see the grooved patterns on their backs,
those soft-souled, toothless creatures
with alien eyes
whose only defense is their hard shells.

A Safe Distance

Sitting by the campfire,
I watch a daddy long legs spider
crawl up my shin.

They are the only spiders I like,
with their long, awkward legs.
I used to play with them
at Nana's camp on Lake Mascoma,
in the dusty shed beside the house
while I watched Daddy work
in the yard.
He never knew I was there.

Last week someone told me that
daddy long legs spiders bite,
but their legs are too long to reach you.

2

Playing Possum

I should be sewing the loose button on
my yellow cardigan
but I'm not.
The cat sleeps so soundly
under the blanket on my lap that
sometimes I think he has died.

Driving home from work
I imagine the discarded canvas bag
at the side of the road
contains body parts.
Even avoiding the news and negative people
it's hard not to be gruesome.
The stories seep into your days,
sensational, sad, told in the hushed tones
of the next victims.

Last night I surprised a possum on the deck.
In the dim porch light
I watched his slow-motion escape
across the snow drifts.
I thought I saw him grinning.

Get a Grip

I lay in bed this morning,
aware of my heart muscle beating,
my lungs filling with air,
inspiring, expiring,
blood racing around
in its busy little vessels –
so many things that have to go right
just to stay alive.

Ann Landers is dead
and her sister has Alzheimer's –
to whom shall we turn?
My head is filled with swirling debris,
and I can't shake that dread
of crossing the center line.
I turn on the car radio –
Jesse Colin Young is singing
"Fear's the way we die."

In the bathroom here
at Greer's Laundromat
the automated paper towel dispenser
sounds like a woman screaming;
The double-loader agitates my clothes.
I open my notebook and read
a quote from Gavin Maxwell's
Ring of Bright Water –

"But to be quite alone
where there are no other human beings

is sharply exhilarating;
it is as though some pressure had suddenly
been lifted."

I should have been a cloistered nun,
but it's too late now.

What's in a Name

Wind whips the pine into a frenzy –
dance, it says,
and the pine has no choice.
It is taller than the house,
birds love it, I love it.
I don't know what kind of pine it is —
would I love it more
if I knew its proper name?

Like when you get a pet
that has no name,
just dog, or cat, or horse,
and then you give it a name,
Fido, Fluffy, Firefly.

You call "Fluffy, here Fluffy!" and
Fluffy comes running,
jumps into your lap
and purrs and purrs,
it's such a comfort,
good kitty, good Fluffy.

I hardly ever worry that the pine
will be uprooted in a gale
and land on the house,
piney green branches
sticking through my kitchen window,
like I do about the airplanes
on their flight path overhead
suddenly losing power,

dropping like doom through the air
to crash in flames onto the roof.
But it could happen.

"Here Fluffy, here Fluffy."

Good Luck

All that's left to do
on the jigsaw puzzle
are the dark pieces;
deep greens, black shadows –
this is the hardest part.

If you're lucky,
there will be nuances,
and all you'll need
are patience,
and a good strong light.

Remember all those years ago,
when I thought I was doomed?
How I embraced the refrain
from "Born Under A Bad Sign"?
If it wasn't for bad luck,
I wouldn't have no luck at all.

It wasn't true, because
in spite of everything
here I am,
content with my puzzle –

but those dark pieces,
they're still here too,
aren't they?

Lament

Where did all the mourning doves go?
They used to line the wires
in front of the house,
mourning like crazy.
What did they have to be so sad about?
I could think of a few things,
but you can't really read anyone else's mind.

Last night the airplanes kept me awake,
just some late-night Air Guard maneuvers,
no need to worry. But I did,
living under the airport flight path,
watching the plane lights heading for
my living room window.
Did they scare the doves away?

> *Come Back Little Sheba*
> was such a great movie —
> sometimes I use that line myself
> to call the cat,
> even though that's not his name.
> It was heart-rending
> when Shirley Booth pleaded,
> "Come back Little Sheba…"

I related to Burt Lancaster,
her drunken husband —
actually I related to them both,
as well as to their dog,
Little Sheba who'd run off,
probably sick of their shenanigans.

But what I really want to say is,
Come back little mourning doves,
mourn your birdie hearts out,
here comes another jet,
we may not be long for this world.

9/12/01
Mourning

On a bench facing the ocean at 8:00 a.m.,
the sun relentless in my eyes,
I feel like
whoever Rod Stewart was singing to –
*The morning sun when it's in your face
really shows your age.*
Silent elderly couples surround me;
we all stare at the sea.

Back on the deck outside my room
at the Norseman Motor Inn
I lie on the chaise lounge,
my legs wrapped in a blanket,
watching an old warrior gull float by
on the tidal river.
He's big and bedraggled and looks blind
in one eye.

Yesterday was September 11,
and I spent the day watching
reruns of disaster, the evening
walking the shoreline.
Seagulls huddled on the sand
as darkness descended.
Waves crashed again and again,
and the lighthouse beacon
kept disintegrating
into the night.

3

Life

When the belligerent bee stung my biceps today
it hurt for a long time.
I waited for an allergic reaction that never came.
I'm not allergic but it could happen.
I may be allergic to wheat or dairy
but I'd rather not know.

Instead of an extreme makeover last night,
I used some Natural Instincts hair color.
My hair came out pretty dark but what the heck.
It said Light Brown but I left it on
longer than the instructions on purpose –
and who was going to stop me?

At the Labor Day cookout
I felt like a jerk,
awkward and foolish.
I wonder if anyone noticed, but
they have their own lives.
I was afraid my car would get blocked in,
but there was a big space around me.
Later I watched "Northfork" on video,
one of the dumbest movies I've ever seen;
I watched the whole thing.
At first I waited for it to get better and then
I just lived through it.

Self-Seeking

All during the drive to New Hampshire,
ideas for poems kept occurring,
about middle age, the hawk
swooping toward my windshield,
frozen rivers under cement bridges –
somewhere under the ice
flow my best ideas.

In Mother's new apartment,
the colorful rug from Wal-Mart
fits perfectly, an Indian pattern
with gold, fuchsia,
blue, and green.

Tomorrow we'll get curtains,
sort her tangled jewelry,
organize the jumbled closets,
everything in a shambles
after the fire and the
emergency move across town
from her water-damaged apartment.

I want to help,
that's why I'm here,
but still
I wish I had time to go
walk along the beach, get lost
searching among the scattered stones,
their petrified little souls saying
See me, see me.

Self Esteem

Standing behind
the metal screen door,
the cat hanging over my shoulder,
watching the lightning,
waiting to be electrocuted,
I catch a glimpse of my face
in the mirror beside the door,
lit only by a clear plastic
kitty night-light,
and I think
"I look pretty darn good
in the dark."

Reprieve

When you're going
seventy miles an hour
there's nothing you can do
to help the hapless fawn
poised beside the highway,
so what a leap of the heart
when he bounds back into the trees
away from the deadly metal,
and no wonder he stays with me,
bright, then slowly dimming,
but never dying.

Oh Happy Day

I have hidden the rubber bands
in the storeroom,
hidden them from my cat,
the rubber-band addict.

I am vigilant,
I have visions of elastic
twisting around his little intestines.
There are so many dangers,

and I'm only human;
last night my insides were
twisted sick with dread
because he hadn't moved his bowels
for two days.

My last cat was afflicted
with constipation,
involving enemas,
medications, emergency vet visits,
so much distress –
thank God I never had children.
And how happy I was this morning
to finally see poop in the kitty box.

I don't ask for much.

A Day at the Beach

High tide –
the water creeps closer
with each heave of the sea.
Biting flies appear and attack
my bare legs, my exposed arms.
I don't care,
I'm on vacation.

Refuse-infested plops of dry seaweed
litter the sand;
a siren screams behind the cement
sea wall;
thundering waves almost drown out
the sound of belching motorcycles,
gassy automobiles.

I sit
in my garishly colored
canvas beach chair,
waiting for a rogue wave,
or maybe just a rogue.
There's no hurry,
I'm on vacation,
and those obsessive worries
I brought to the beach
about my aching, disintegrating jaw,
my age-related hearing loss,
my pot belly,
and me, me, me –
all lost at sea.

OK So I'm Not a Genius

What's that genius society
where you have to have
a really high IQ?
I don't know anyone who belongs,
but I think I met one once
when I answered a personal ad for
"The most intelligent woman in the world"
as a joke.

We exchanged letters
and I must have sounded
pretty damn smart.
He agreed to meet at
Uncommon Grounds for coffee;
said I'd know him
by the jade plant he'd be holding.

I found him attractive,
in a haughty genius kind of way;
then he presented
his portfolio of avant-garde sculptures,
expounded on
his philosophy,
his poetry,
his artwork,
the house in the country he had built
himself.

What a show-off.
I didn't have to be a genius

to know he was not
Mr. Right.

I did keep the jade plant –
considered it a rescue.

Like Life

Lying in the sun
for the first time this summer –
there's a cool breeze,
my mind drifts…

Gerry's pink Geraniums thrive
in their window boxes.
She cleaned her porch today,
even washed the stairs,
while I lolled
on my chaise lounge.
I should have felt guilty.

Now the sun is sinking,
my feet are getting cold,
but no problem,
I've brought some socks out.
I've always been the one
who has just what you need,
aspirin, a rubber band,
hand-warmers.
But I've decided to change,
and it's going pretty well –
it helps if I don't carry a purse.

Something's going on
in the gravel pit out back –
not quite as bad
as the blasting that feels
like an earthquake,
just rhythmic thuds.

Ah yes, early evening
and the birds are singing –
so it's

Tra la la   thud
Tra la la   thud
Tra la la   thud,
like life.

Voices

A winter hike,
crystal snow flashing
pink and blue
under the blazing sun.

The group's petite
white-haired leader lectured,
pointing out footprints of coyote,
fox, and vole;
the others talked, talked
and talked,
full of their travels to Italy,
France,
and Utah.

I dropped back,
ducked off the trail,
put more distance between us,
and bushwhacked down the hill
through mute winter woods
to the water's edge
where the brook,
its voice muffled,
churned and tumbled,
hidden under thick aqua ice.

Bare Ground

I can hear the telephone ringing
but I am unavailable,
sitting naked on the toilet
in the steamy bathroom,
filing my nails.

I can think of one person
for whom I'd run dripping
to answer the phone,
but he doesn't know it.
It's my little secret,
just like everything else.

I keep my nails short
and harmless.
My hair is *too* short —
I tug at my bangs, but it's no use,
I'll just have to wait.
In the meantime,
Hideo Nomo pitched a no-hitter
today in his Red Sox debut.
It's all downhill for him now.

In my figure drawing class,
I seemed to regress
as the weeks went on.
It was that last model's fault —
too thin to sink your pencil into.
The first one
was eight months pregnant –

it was so much fun
drawing those big circles.

Lately, I've seen a robin
and a red-winged blackbird,
heard the mourning dove,
smelled a skunk;
Spring is finally here,
and this bare ground
won't last long.

4

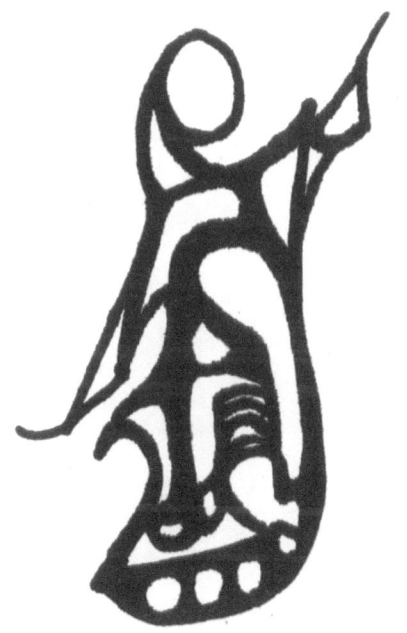

Therapy

That distant
sweltering summer,
after the overdose,
I awoke from the coma
with a droopy right eye
and a weird sensitivity
on the side of my neck.

Recovering at home,
lying motionless,
a heat lamp on my bedsore,
I listened to CHOM,
the Canadian station –
Van Morrison, Neil Young,
Derek and the Dominos.

For my paralyzed right arm,
the Occupational Therapist
prescribed wiping off tables
and kitchen counters,
or dusting with a circular motion.
How did she know
what a mess our apartment was?

My boyfriend Michael,
the heroin addict,
wasn't around much,
but every so often he'd come home,
hang around for a while,
sometimes tickle my neck

to make me laugh —
maybe his idea of therapy.

Today,
the cat sprawls limply on my lap,
wiped out by the heat.
In the garden
the Larkspurs have blossomed,
the Asters
just have a lot of leaves –
at least they're still alive.

You win some,
lose some.

Love Sick

At Klinger's Bakery
Stephen Stills' "Love the One You're With"
is playing in the background.

The last time I heard that song
was in 1970,
on the way to Johnson State College
with Michael
for some sort of drug transaction –
heroin, speed, liquid opium –
God only knows what it was that day,
I didn't care, I just wanted to be
with Michael,
but he was bisexual
and I only ever had
half his attention.
I was love sick and drug sick
and I went along for the ride,
loving the one I was with,
not exactly happy, but
close enough.

What ever happened to Stephen Stills?

Seeing the Light

Colchester, Vermont:
Four in the morning,
I lie on my back on the deck,
waiting for the Leonid Meteor Shower.

Portsmouth, New Hampshire:
After closing the bar
I found myself lying
half-dressed in the snow
outside the Seacoast Village apartment
of a man I'd gone home with.

I must have seemed like easy pickings –
I thought I was, too – but changed my mind:
something about The Beatles'
Fool On The Hill on the stereo,
or his rough hands.
He called me "frigid,"
and pushed me out the door,
into the icy embrace of the snow,
where I lay exposed by the bright porch light.

Burlington, Vermont:
I woke up wasted at three a.m.
in a dim, dirty room above the Red Dog Bar
with my roommate Doris
and five band members,
wondering what I had done.

Trying to walk home I
fell flat on the foul slushy sidewalk

wailing "I want to go home"
while my friends disappeared
and a policeman shone his flashlight
in my face.

Those days I kept my head down,
my eyes on the ground.

This morning,
in my pink flannel nightgown,
sweatpants, and purple parka,
I look up,
and see sixteen shooting stars
in the clean, cold dawn.

All Is Not Lost

Last night I dreamed
I could play the violin —
just picked it up and started playing
"Mary Had A Little Lamb."

I wish I still had the guitar
Mother bought me in Boston
when I was sixteen.
I could play by ear,
but my cat would run from the room
if I started singing.

I kept it through high school,
my failed attempt at college,
my first disastrous marriage —

and then what?

Did I sell it for drugs, give it away
in a fit of alcoholic generosity,
or just carelessly leave it behind
one of the fifteen times I moved?
Gone, gone, gone,
part of a litany of loss
like my dog,
my suede mini-skirt,
my self-respect.

Maybe Mother
should have bought me
a violin, but never mind,

things are different now,
all is not lost,
and I could always buy myself
a used guitar somewhere,
start again.

Lower Companion

That Thanksgiving
at your parents' house on Park Street
is one reason your mother never liked me.

Already primed with wine when we arrived,
I tried to help you pull the table apart
for the extra leaf and lost my grip, landing
sprawled on my back on the kitchen floor
at the feet of your horrified mother.

A disapproving pall settled in
for the rest of the day;
I spent the rest of the long afternoon
after a meal I don't remember
sitting meekly on the sofa, pretending
to watch football, longing for a cigarette
and a pick-me-up.

She thought I was a bad influence
and she had a point –
I was one of the "lower companions"
that drinkers seek out
so as not to appear so depraved themselves.

You did come to a bad end, of course,
discovered by your twin brother
hanging in the closet of your ground-floor flat
on Monroe Street,
and though I didn't blame myself,
I couldn't face your mother at the funeral

so I didn't go,
and that still haunts me.

You're buried in the cemetery on Archibald Street.
I don't think I could find your grave now
after so many years, and, after all,
why dig up the past?

The Guilty Ones

At first I blamed the ants infesting the garden,
but they could not have caused such destruction;
it's the rabbits that freeze in my headlights at night,
and the trembling deer I see from my window
crossing the lawn at dawn.

They used to stay
in the fields and woods behind the house
before bulldozers gouged and flattened the land.
Now, while I sleep, they feast
on my lettuce, spinach, nasturtiums,
the tender leaves of the tomatoes.

Evenings I climb the hill to the garden,
wondering what they have left me,
what will be cropped close to the ground.

God knows I haven't always been harmless –
sins of omission, sins of commission, the nights
John lay alone and angry, wondering,
while I cruised the dark bars with my friends.

So forgive us our trespasses,
and go ahead and eat,
my fellow hungry creatures.
There are worse kinds of damage.

Some People Need To Be Taught a Lesson

What fun we had that summer night, Jim, Gerry and I,
trying to decapitate the parking meters
in front of our building on Bank Street,
taking turns
      BANG BANG BANG
with a pipe wrench, laughing hysterically,
boy those things are built to last.

So we gave it up and ran
across the street to the grassy hill, where we
rolled down, crawled back up, rolled down,
till we lay on our grass-stained backs at the bottom
shrieking with laughter –
oh sure we'd been drinking,
of course we were drinking –
but one of the neighbors called the cops.
All of a sudden there they were, looming,
and they weren't laughing.
They didn't arrest us, just laid down the law.

A little subdued, we staggered back home
where Michael, my glowering boyfriend waited,
and I made some snide remark like
What a wet blanket!
so he pushed me down the stairs,
but I showed him,
shattered the front door glass with my fist.
Really taught him a lesson.

On This First Hot Day in April

In from the garden,
I stand at the sink
washing my hands
and contemplate the wildlife
on my kitchen windowpane –
a ladybug, a fly, a spider.
We co-exist as long as they
know their place; otherwise,
they are doomed.

I once knew a man
who shot himself,
after first pointing the gun at us,
his friends, then
at the officers called to help,
then at his head.

He'd been acting strangely,
pouring milk on bologna in a bowl,
putting his head in the gas oven;
he had the Thorazine shuffle.
He would only go to the beach with us
if he could take his bottle of gin.
There was nothing left inside.

Once, he'd been an artist,
clever and creative;
we were fellow boozers, pals.
A friend of ours once said,
"When Gerry drinks,

he's fun to be around,
but you are like
Dr. Jekyll and Mr. Hyde."

He wouldn't have recognized me
today, all these years later
in my sun hat,
on this first, hot, healing day in April,
in the garden
on my knees
burying seeds.

Haunted

My new clothes hamper
is still in the car
while I wait in my apartment
for the rain to stop.

My cat shredded the old one –
white wicker —
I don't remember where I got it,
though I'm sure it was second-hand,
or third.

Some things I found in basements
of places where I lived,
like the metal stands
I keep my plants on,
or the big wood-framed mirror
in the bedroom.

Those were from the haunted house
where my husband
and our friend who lived upstairs
killed themselves,
months apart.

I walked by that place last summer,
thirty years later –
its ugly dirt-patch front yard,
its broken blinds –
and even in the sunshine, with flowers
all around everywhere else,
it gave me a chill.

But nothing like that
would ever happen here;
it's all behind me now.

As far as I can see
it's all behind me now.

Substitution

"Sixteen Tons" comes on the radio,
the old Tennessee Ernie Ford tune.
I remember singing along with Ernie
when I was ten,
on the floor of my bedroom at Nana's house,
working on some project requiring glue,
busy, busy, busy…
Much of my childhood is a blank,
but that scene has stayed —
probably etched into my brain
by the fumes.

It turned out that glue
was not my drug of choice after all,
just a precursor to the solvent alcohol
that made everything keep falling apart.

That's all gone now, but still, I love
the invigorating fragrance of gasoline,
the occasional essence
of magic marker, paint-thinner,
nail-polish remover,
the melancholy, smoky aftermath of
extinguished candles;

a blown-out match.

Drunks and Fools

Another Sunday evening, getting dark.
The cat stands undecided on the coffee table –
to get on my lap, to not get on my lap.
He places one paw on the blanket, hesitates,
another paw, walks across my legs,
and off again.

Earlier, I watched
Brother Sun, Sister Moon
about St. Francis of Assisi,
soundtrack by Donovan.
I used to have one of his albums
when I lived in Portsmouth
after the divorce,
with my protective German Shepherd,
and three long-suffering cats, rescued
from the vet's where I worked.
Sometimes for a treat
I'd cook them up a mess of
frozen smelt.

For my treat I'd take the bus
to the nearest convenience store
to buy as much Pabst Blue Ribbon
as I could carry,
and some Marlboros.
Thank God for my record player,
and cheap beer;
all I did besides work was drink
and listen to records,

maybe sing along with Donovan, Dylan
or the Beatles –
> *The fool on the hill sees the sun going down...*

Things ended badly there,
myself on the psych ward,
my dog given to strangers,
my cats back in cages.

Now, this cat comes back,
curls up beside me.
Severe wind chill advisory tonight,
but I am safe inside, listening to
the windows rattle and whine harmlessly.
And today, a different sun has gone down
on a life so normal, so peaceful,
so like a daydream.

5

Dream On

At Starbucks last night
I smiled at the cute guy with a laptop
at the table next to me.
Sometimes I can be so pathetic.
I know some men like older women;
they must have found them already.

Last night I dreamed I was in
a public toilet with no electricity.
At my age, I can't sleep the whole night
without getting up at least once in the dark.
The snooze button on my digital alarm
gives me nine more minutes every morning –
it's never enough.
Things are starting to wear down.
If I don't get a massage soon,
my head will break off at the neck.

I'm practically blind driving at night –
my vision plays tricks on me.
Suddenly I'll think I see something
out of the corner of my eye,
something moving too quickly.
If I had my way
I'd stay home every evening with my
co-dependent cat
who doesn't know how old I am.

Night before last I dreamed that
the brakes on my Toyota Matrix failed.
At a red light I couldn't stop

no matter how hard I tried,
until I stood with my whole weight
on the brake and still,
we rolled inexorably forward.

Let's Face It
    (After reading poems by David Budbill)

I sit
at a marble-topped table
at Nunyun's bakery
chugging French Roast coffee
from a white mug,
reading poems by a man
who talks about his face sliding off,
and grey hair,
and I say "Me too!"
Though actually at the moment
my hair is kind of
a dark mahogany brown,
after my hairdresser said,
"Let me color your hair
For your 65th birthday."
And though it came out too dark
I like it anyway,
what the hell,
who cares if I want to look younger
for six weeks,
which is how long it takes the color
to fade, unlike youth,
which takes longer,
but eventually, yes,
your face does start to slide off,
no matter what color your hair is.

Window-Box, Snack Mix

It probably means nothing
that I keep losing words.
Composing an email about
the flowers on my balcony,
the word for "window-box"
was gone;
not for good, of course,
it came to me eventually,
a very long eventually,
as I sat with my head in my hands,
my mind a blank.

Last week there was
a scary spell of sickness
that woke me at one a.m.
at New Discovery Campground.
It might have been something I ate,
but I made the mistake
when I got home
of looking up "Heart-Attack Symptoms"
on the Internet.
My Stress Test appointment is this week.

Shopping for groceries last night
I stood in front of the Cheesy Snack Mix
for what seemed like forever,
trying to talk myself out of
wasting money on disgusting junk food,
until finally I came to my senses and said
Oh lighten up,

*just get the damn snack mix,
you'll be dead soon anyway!*

No matter how you define soon.

Yoga Moment

I couldn't be the only person
who's ever farted in a yoga class.
Thank God the room was dim
and a recording of birds chirping
played in the background.
Usually I prefer silence, but tonight
I was grateful for that distraction.

I felt off-center –
I was jealous of the woman to my left,
who has yet another boyfriend and
is tanned and glowing from their
recent Tropical Cruise,
and the snooty young girl to my right
who bends into impossible postures
without effort, and has perfect balance.

I'll bet they heard me.

Windows

I've seen this Antiques Roadshow,
so I turn off the TV.
The windows are open,
I hear birds,
I can't identify their calls
but I know a bird when I hear one.
I have a few antiques from Mother,
the rest is yard sale;
will anyone want my possessions?

It's still light out.
the cat perches on the windowsill,
mesmerized by the birds.
A blue glass fish lies broken on the floor,
knocked off its hook last night
when I opened the blinds.
I meant to pick it up,
but I've become absent-minded.

Once, when she was 80,
I asked Mother if she still worried
about how she looked, and
yes, the answer was yes.
I'm already tired of holding in my stomach,
my sacroiliac aches, my left shoulder
is disintegrating.

But I'm pretty well-adjusted, considering,
until I contemplate the coming cold,
the dark,
and the closing of the windows.

The Bright Side

Unpaid bills litter the kitchen table;
the sun forces itself through clouds
briefly before retreating;
the Privet hedge needs clipping.

My back has been out of joint
since I wrenched it at work
lifting a stack of charts.
If I sit too long in one place
it really starts to hurt,
which makes it hard
to watch the Red Sox
for any length of time.

I try to have a positive attitude.
Like last night when I banged my head
on the plastic toilet seat
while putting lotion on my legs,
my first thought was *Thank God
it wasn't the porcelain tub!*
And at the car wash,
where I can do anything I want
in the dark forest of pink and blue
side-slapping spongy strips,
near the final rinse I yell,
I see the light at the end of the tunnel!

Lay Lady Lay
   (Song from Bob Dylan's *Nashville Skyline* album)

In my Hippie days,
nobody had a real bed.
We all crashed on mattresses
on the floor,
and everyone wore their hair long,
parted in the middle,
framing our friendly faces.

We shared joints
and boxes of Oreos,
listened to Crosby, Stills & Nash,
slept with the nearest
available warm body.

Sometimes, on my way to work,
I'll drive down Loomis Street, past
the big white apartment house
where I first did acid with Rick.

We lay on the floor all night,
tripping to Bob Dylan's
Nashville Skyline, playing it
over and over and over –
far out.

Sometimes I wonder,
how did I end up
sleeping alone
in this queen-size bed,
on the straight and narrow
with a pixie cut?

www.ingramcontent.com/pod-product-compliance
Lightning Source LLC
Chambersburg PA
CBHW020623300426
44113CB00007B/760